STAR WARS

FOR CLASSICAL GUITAR

Arranged by Pete Billmann and Jeff Jacobson

ISBN 978-1-4950-5886-8

Visit Hal Leonard Online at
www.halleonard.com

Contact us:
Hal Leonard
7777 West Bluemound Road
Milwaukee, WI 53213
Email: info@halleonard.com

In Europe, contact:
Hal Leonard Europe Limited
42 Wigmore Street
Marylebone, London, W1U 2RN
Email: info@halleonardeurope.com

In Australia, contact:
Hal Leonard Australia Pty. Ltd.
4 Lentara Court
Cheltenham, Victoria, 3192 Australia
Email: info@halleonard.com.au

Star Wars
(Main Theme)

from STAR WARS: A NEW HOPE

Music by John Williams

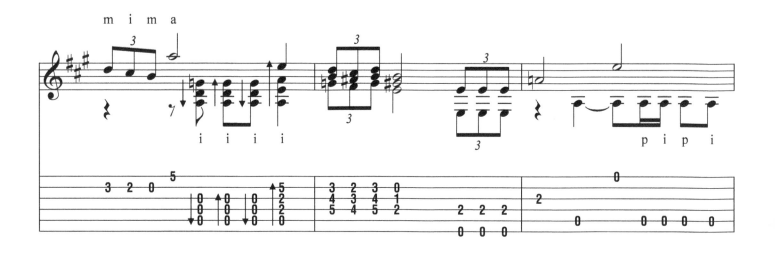

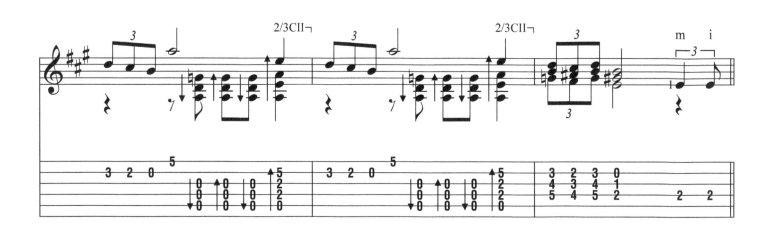

Cantina Band

from STAR WARS: A NEW HOPE
Music by John Williams

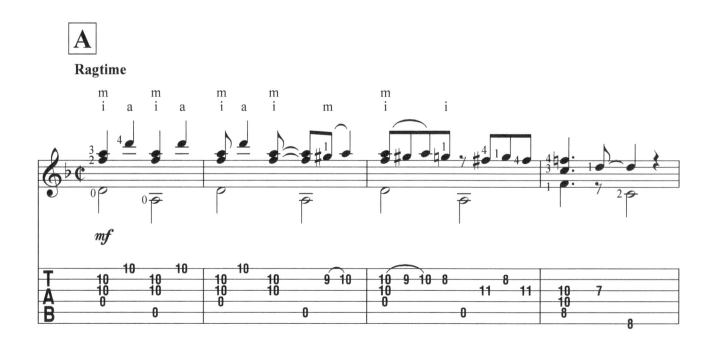

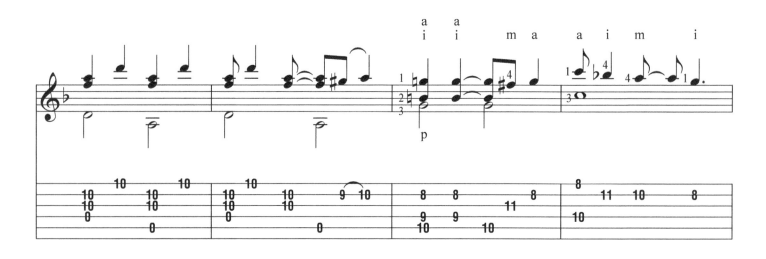

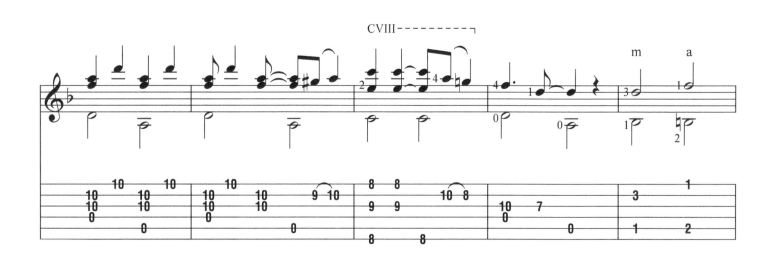

To Coda ⊕

B

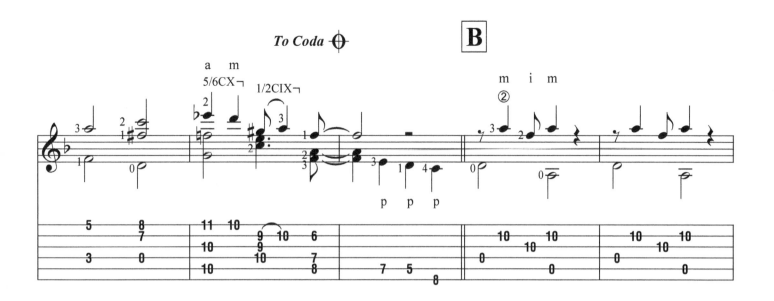

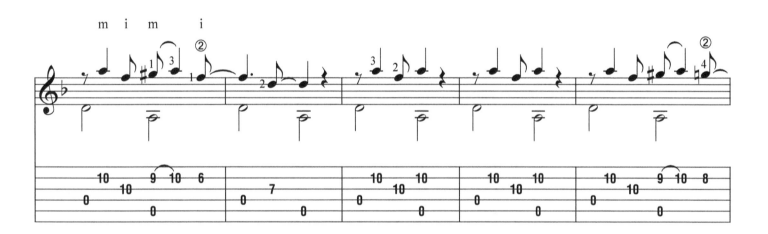

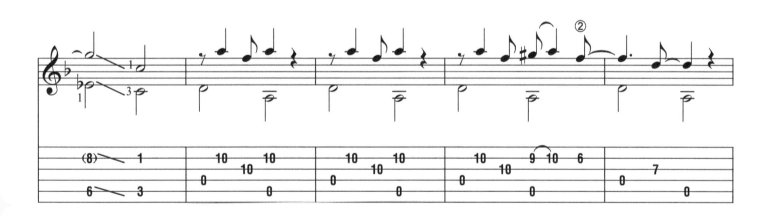

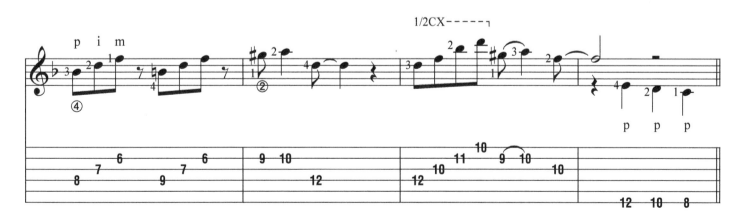

C

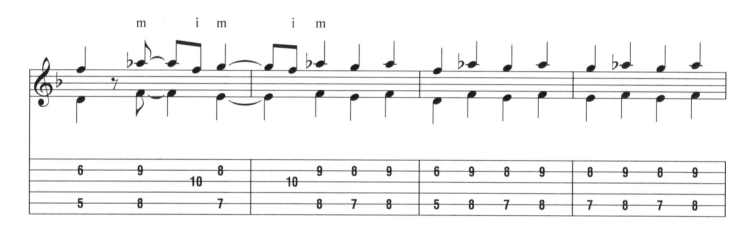

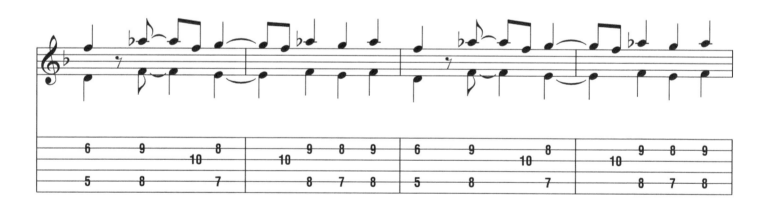

D.C. al Coda   ⊕ **Coda**

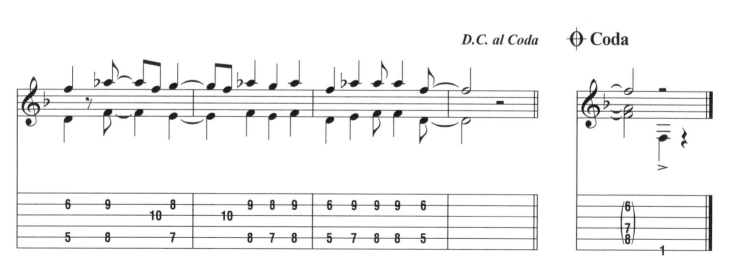

Across the Stars

(Love Theme from *STAR WARS: ATTACK OF THE CLONES*)

Music by John Williams

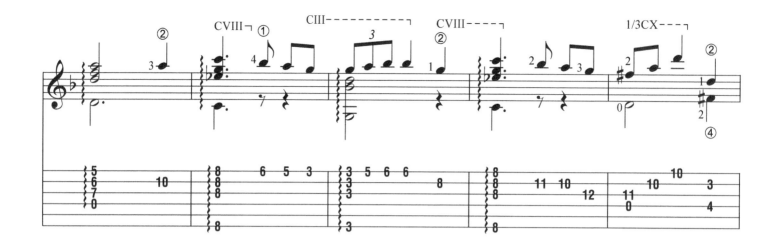

C

D

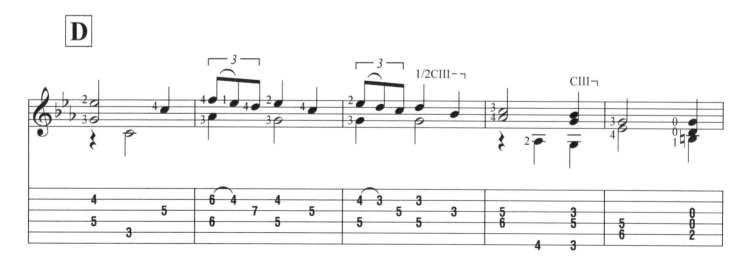

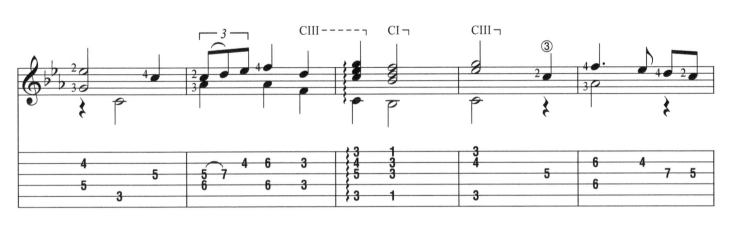

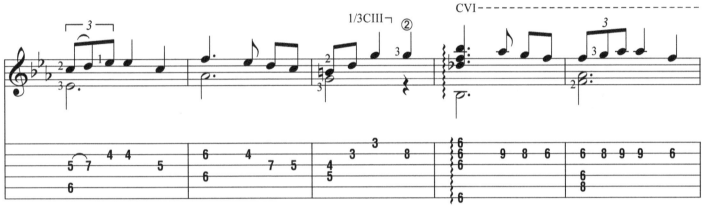

E

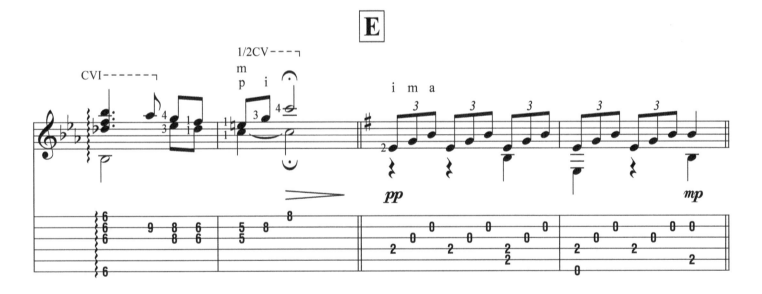

F

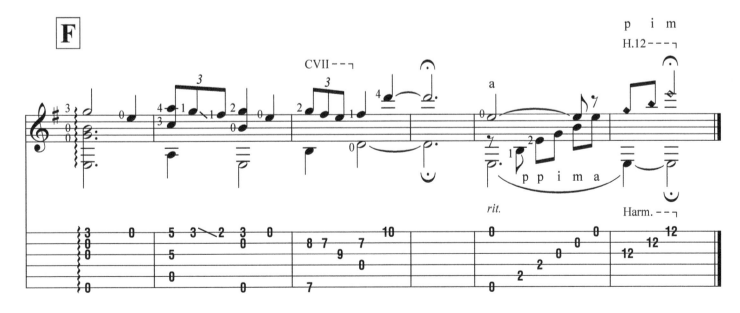

Han Solo and the Princess

from STAR WARS: THE EMPIRE STRIKES BACK

Music by John Williams

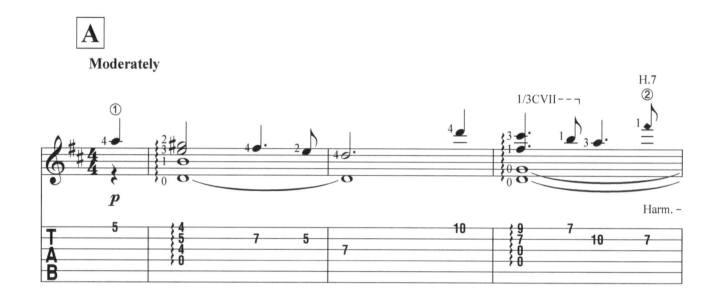

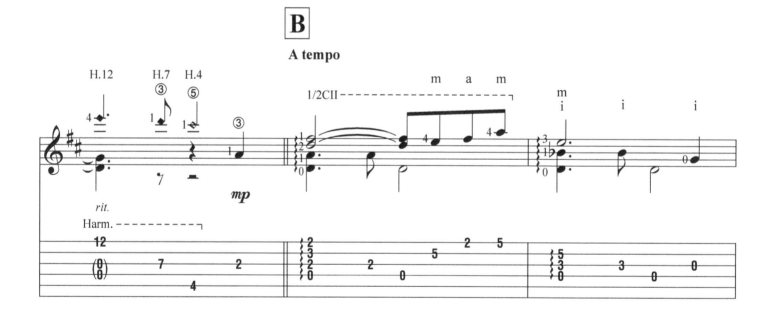

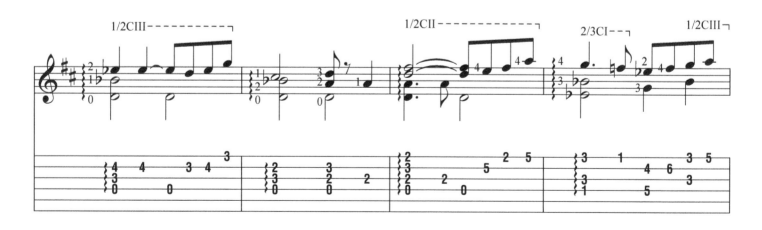

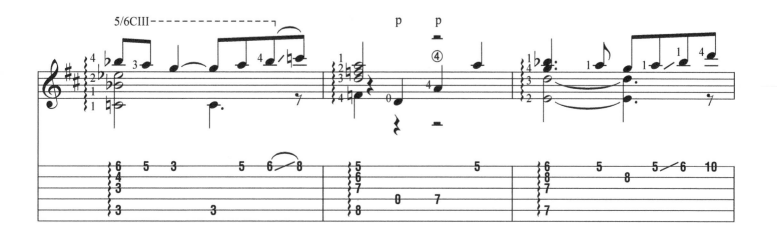

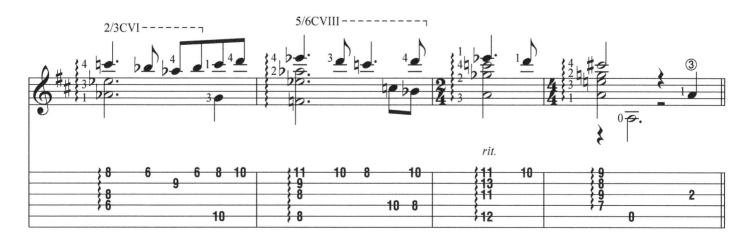

C

A tempo

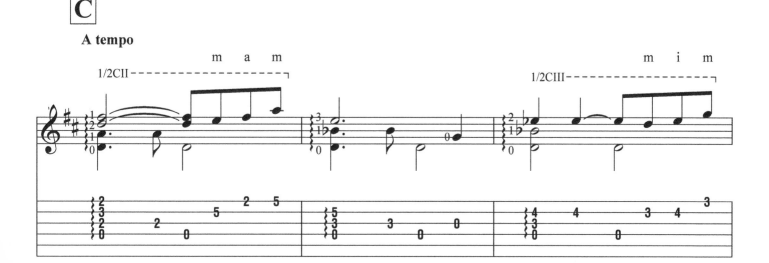

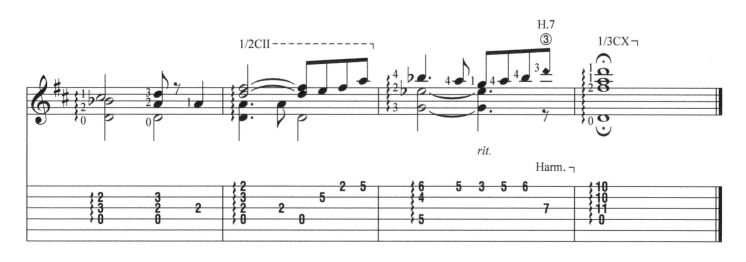

The Imperial March

(Darth Vader's Theme)

from STAR WARS: THE EMPIRE STRIKES BACK

Music by John Williams

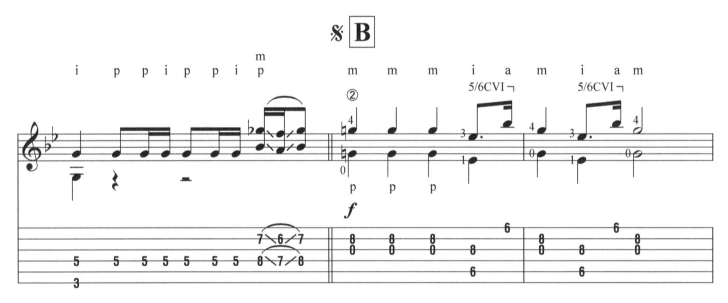

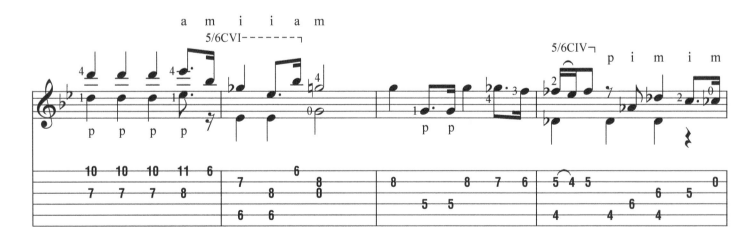

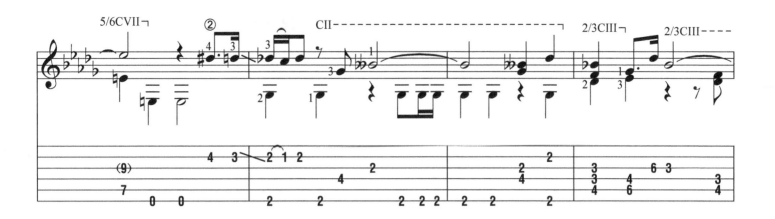

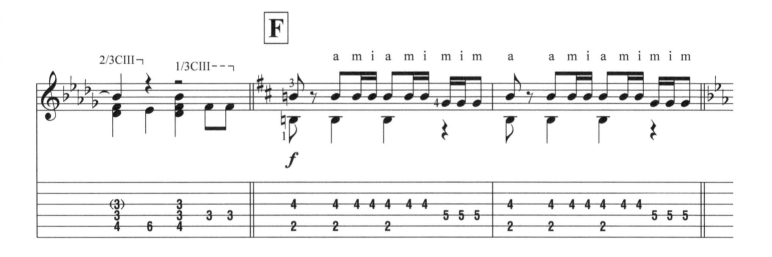

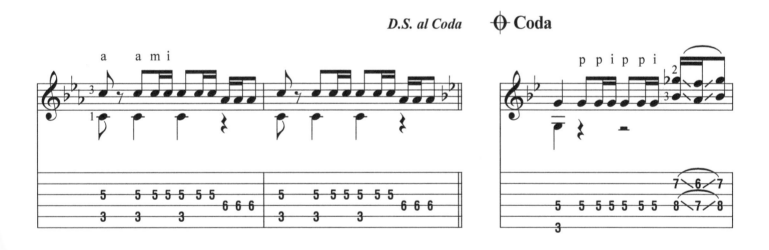

The Jedi Steps *and* Finale

from STAR WARS: THE FORCE AWAKENS

Music by John Williams

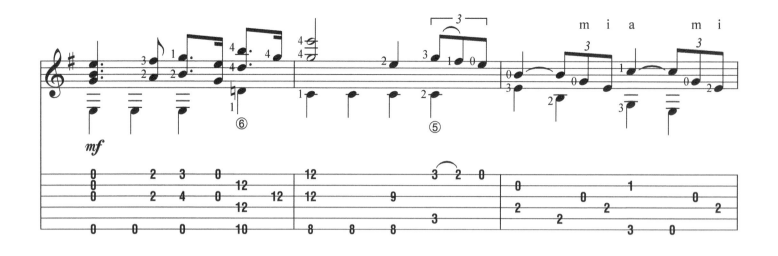

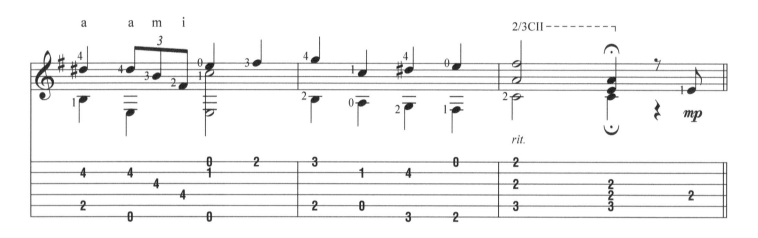

E

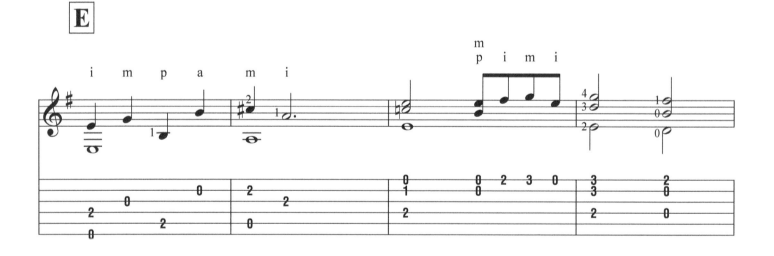

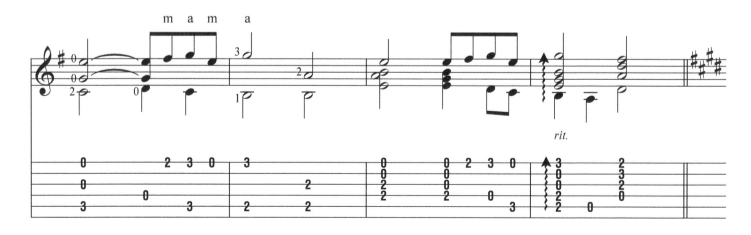

March of the Resistance

from STAR WARS: THE FORCE AWAKENS

Music by John Williams

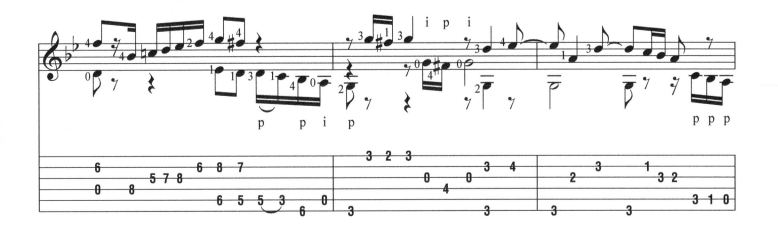

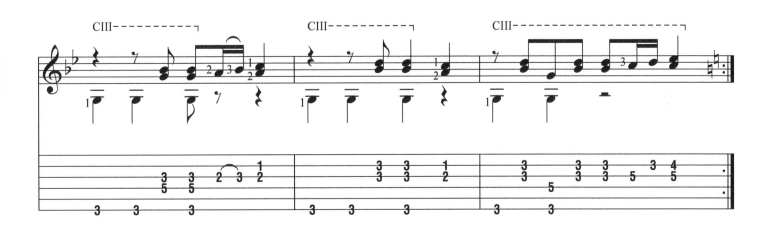

C

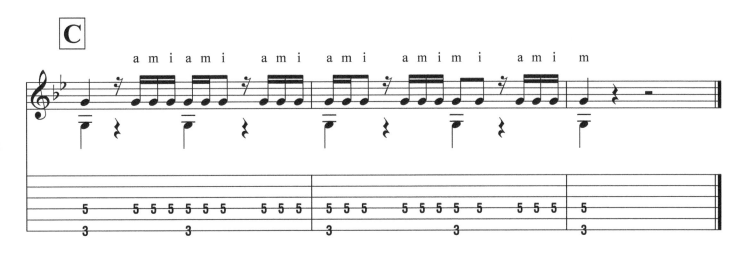

Princess Leia's Theme

from STAR WARS: A NEW HOPE

Music by John Williams

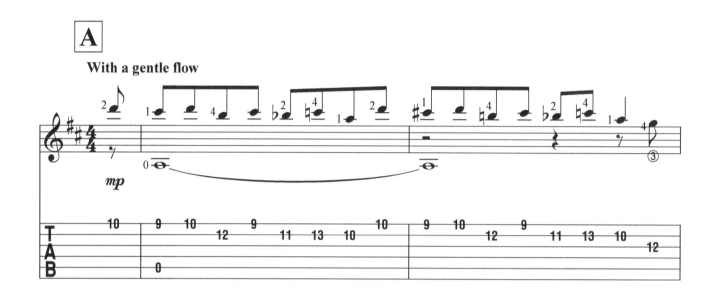

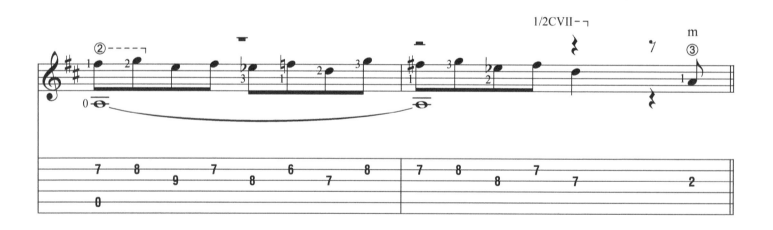

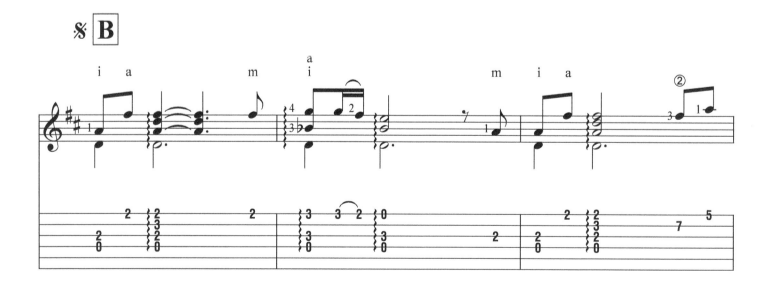

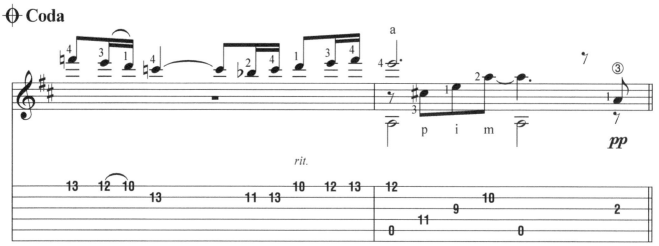

Coda

D

A tempo

Duel of the Fates

from STAR WARS: THE PHANTOM MENACE

Music by John Williams

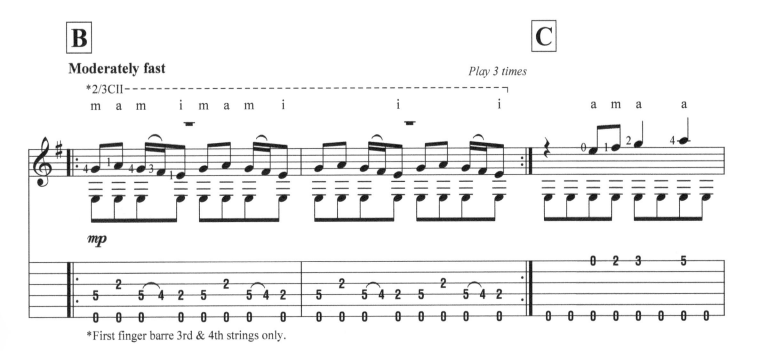

*First finger barre 3rd & 4th strings only.

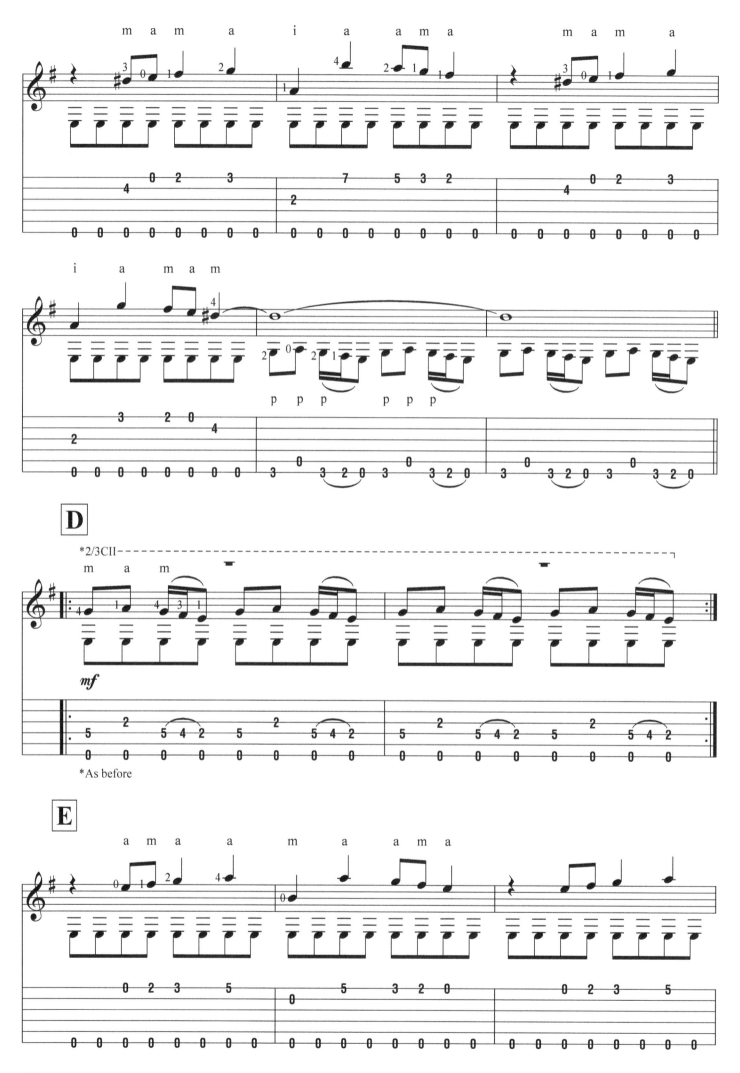

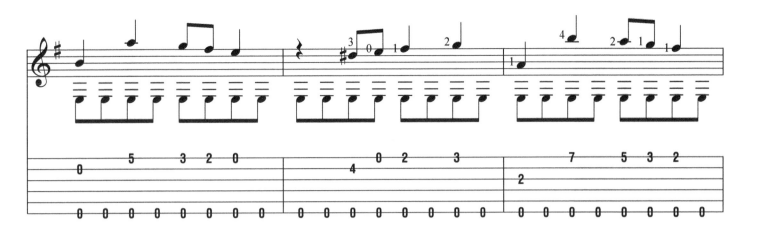

*As before

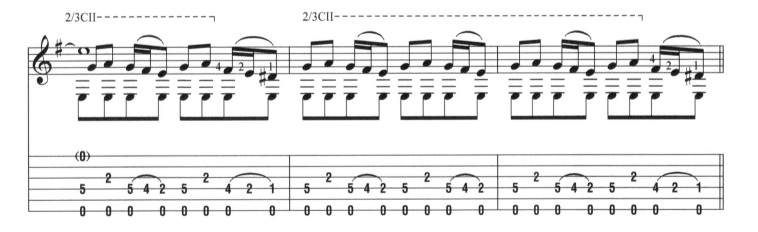

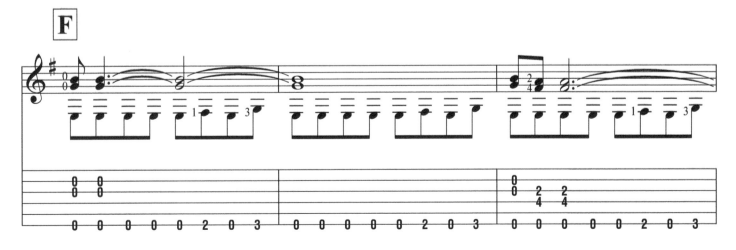

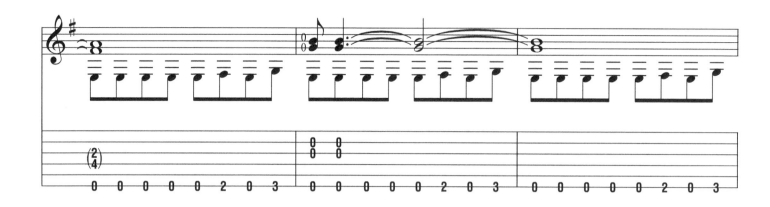

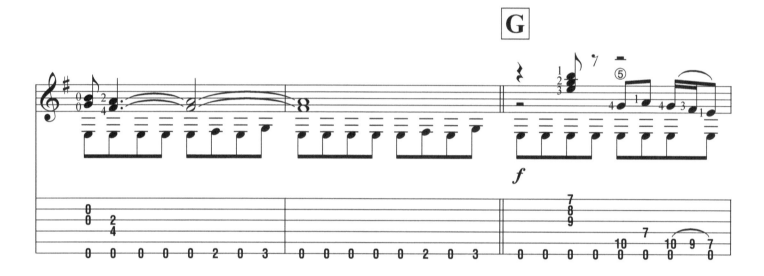

G

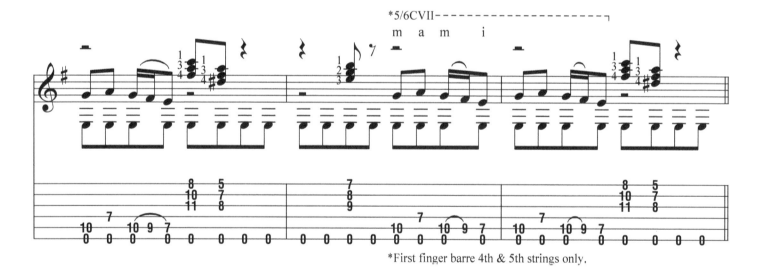

*5/6CVII

*First finger barre 4th & 5th strings only.

H

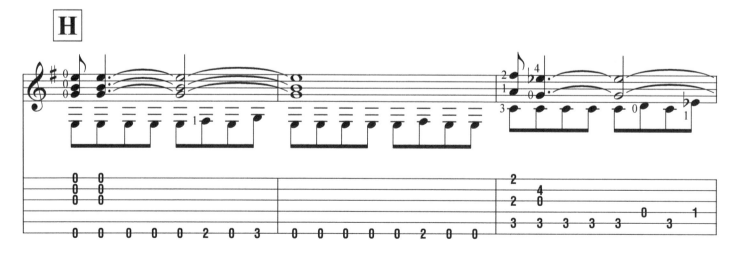

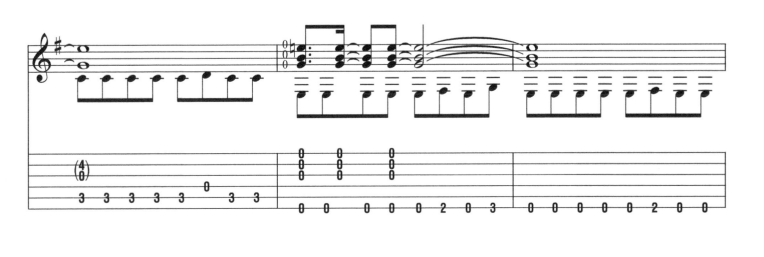

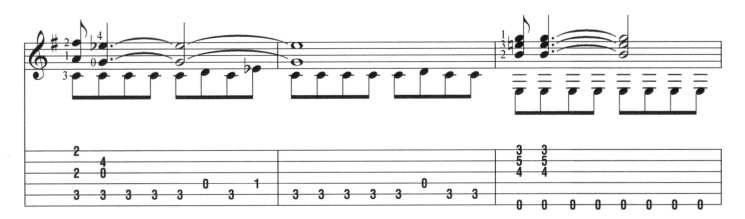

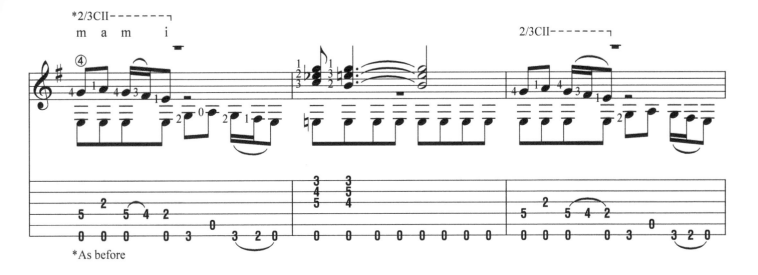

*As before

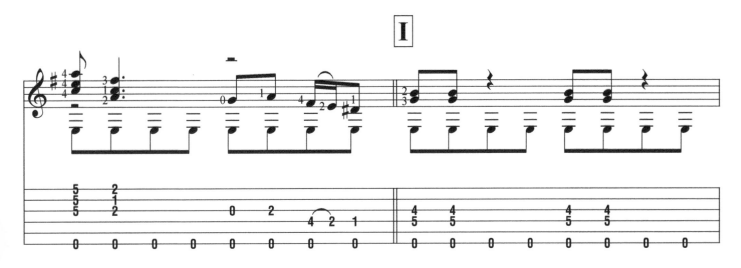

Rey's Theme

from STAR WARS: THE FORCE AWAKENS

Music by John Williams

A

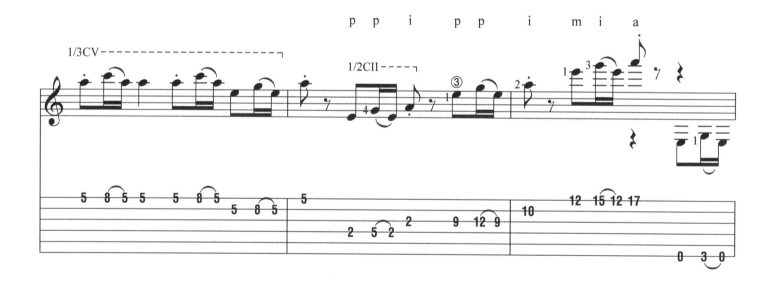

B

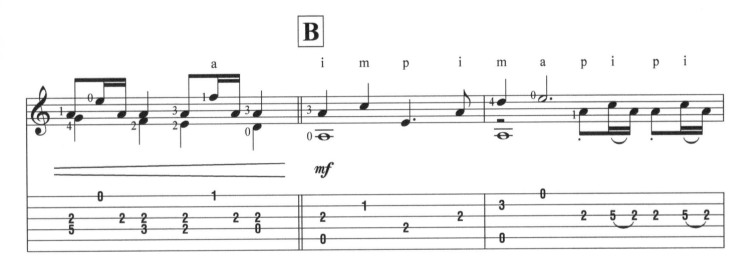

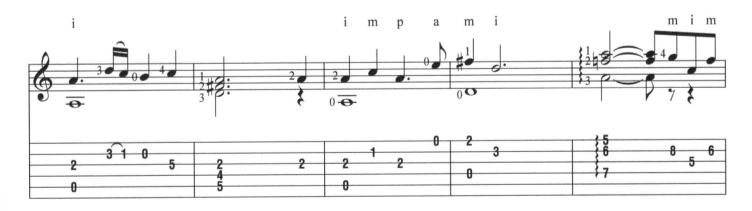

To Coda ⊕

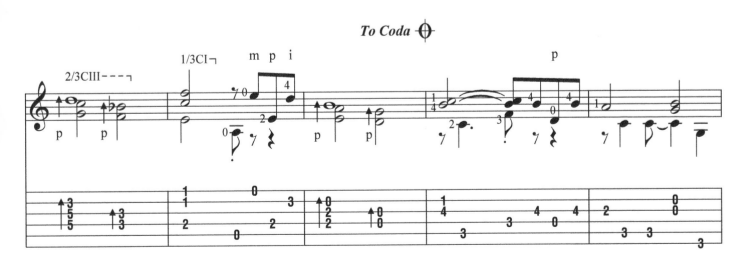

⊕ **Coda**

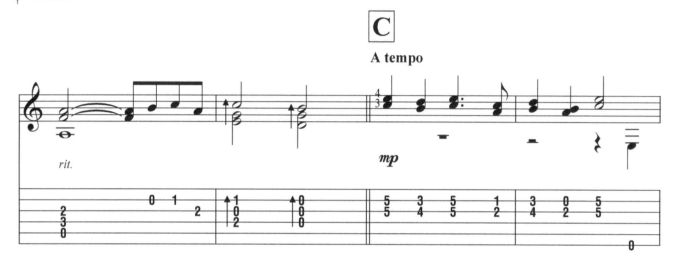

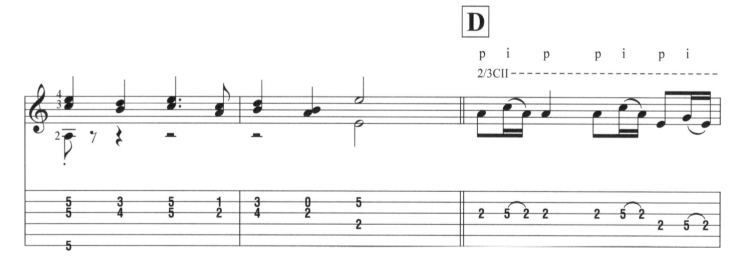

Luke and Leia

from STAR WARS: RETURN OF THE JEDI

Music by John Williams

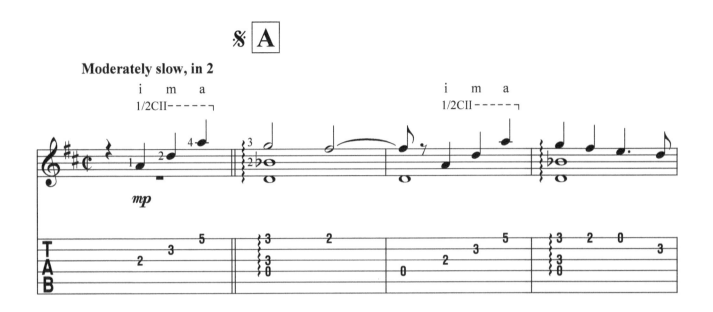

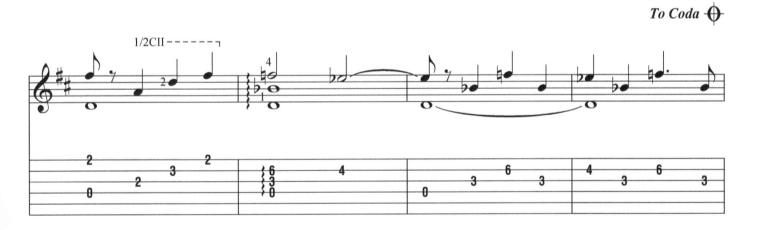

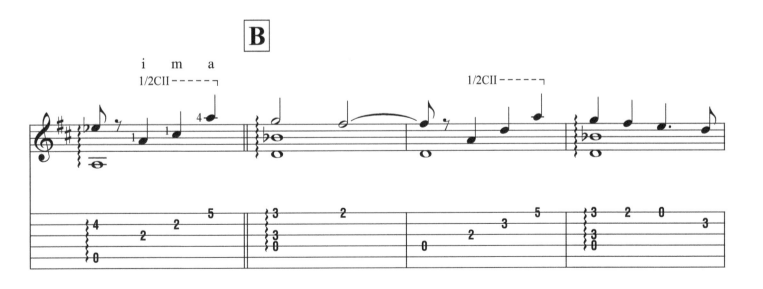

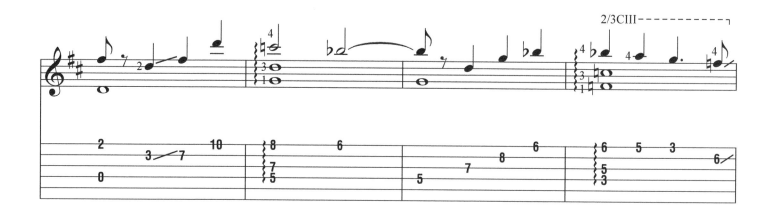

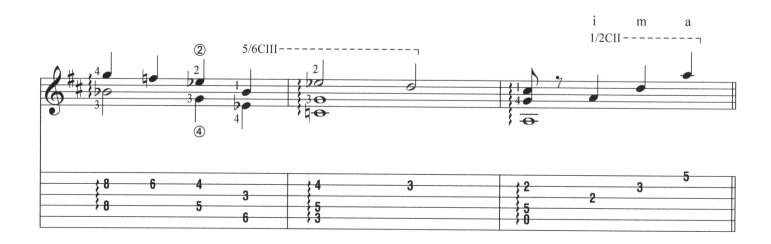

C

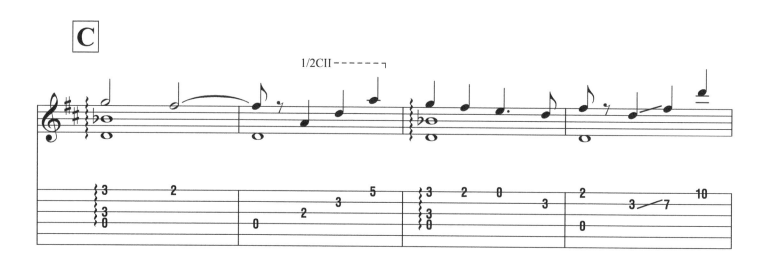

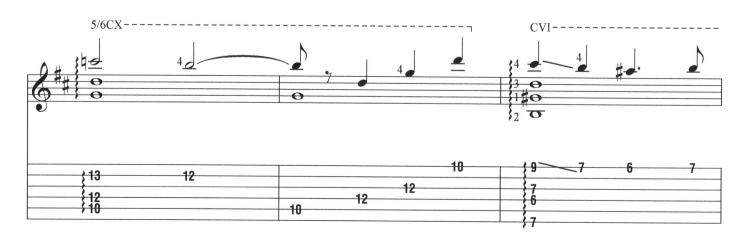

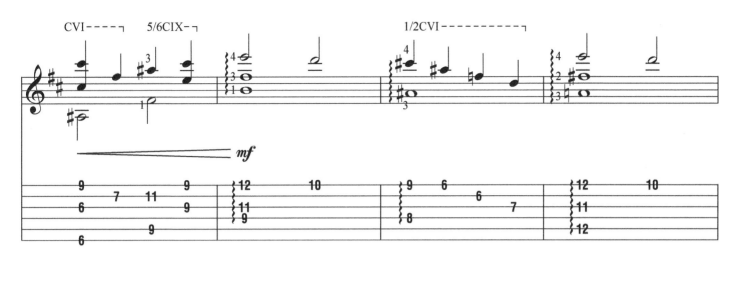

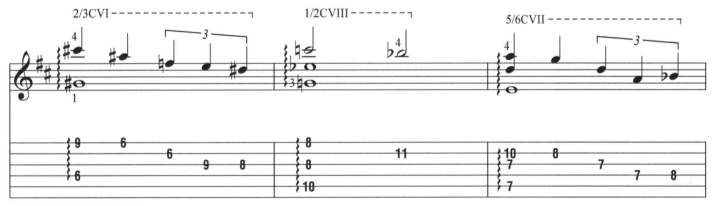

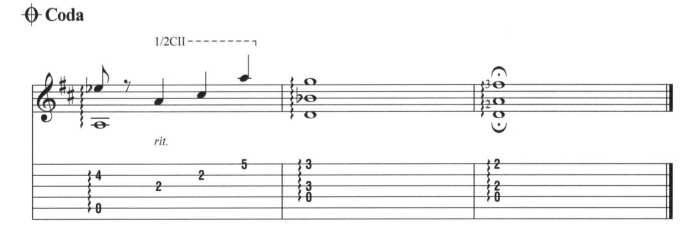

Yoda's Theme

from STAR WARS: THE EMPIRE STRIKES BACK
Music by John Williams

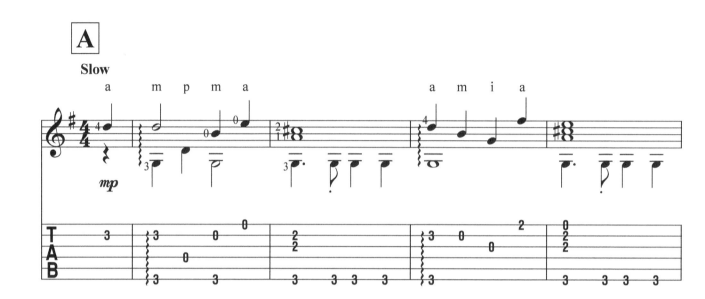

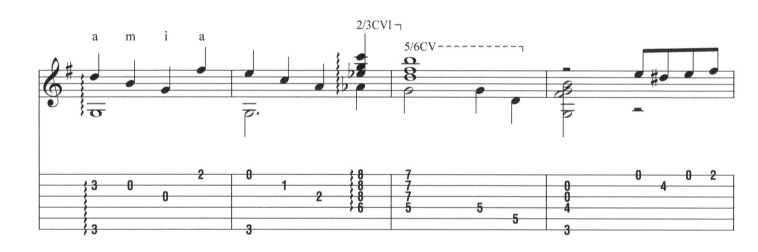

*Refers to fifth fret notes only.

May the Force Be with You

from STAR WARS: A NEW HOPE

Music by John Williams

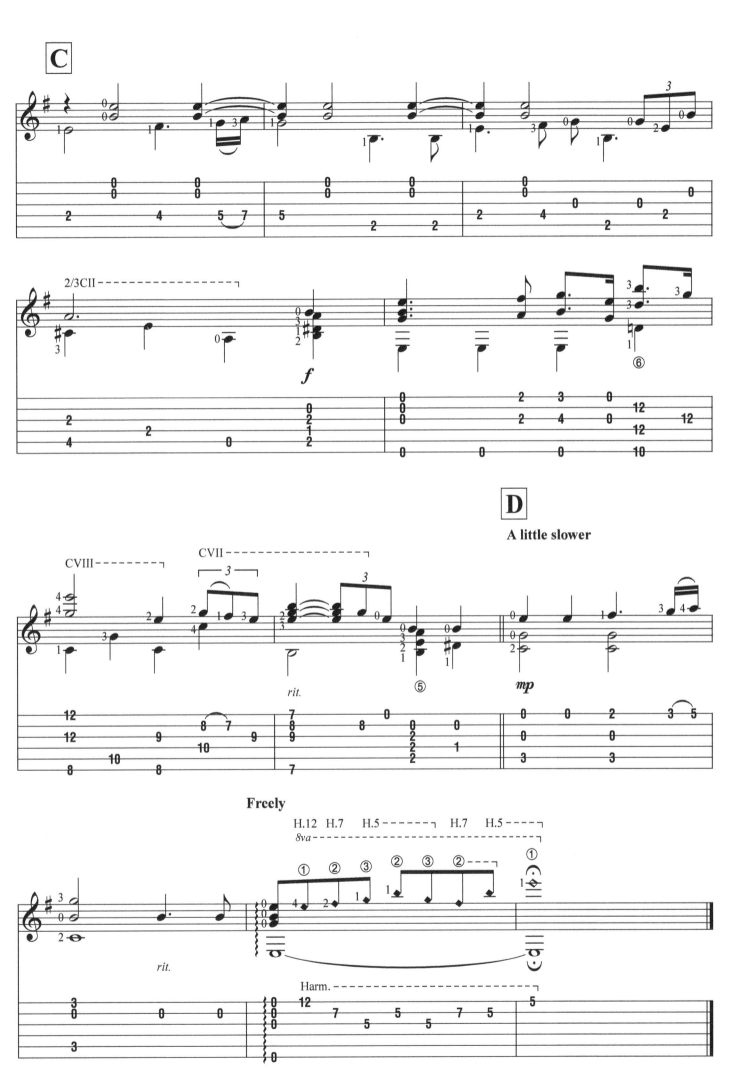

The Throne Room *and* End Title

from STAR WARS: A NEW HOPE

Music by John Williams

A

Majestically

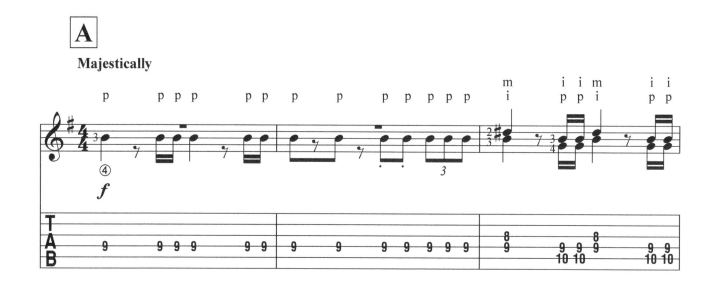

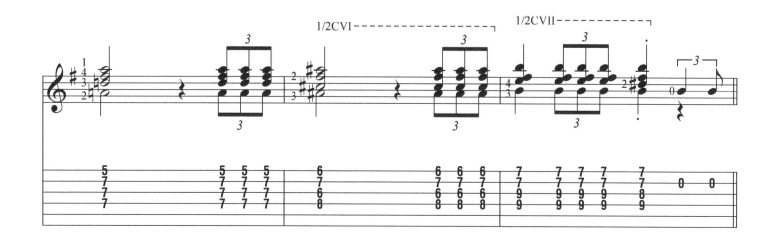

Classical Guitar Repertoire
AVAILABLE NOW FROM HAL LEONARD

The Beatles for Classical Guitar
31 of the Beatles' best arranged for solo classical guitar in standard notation and tablature. Includes: Across the Universe • Blackbird • Eleanor Rigby • The Fool on the Hill • Hey Jude • Michelle • Norwegian Wood • Something • Yesterday • and more.
00699237...$22.99

Classic Rock for Classical Guitar
arr. John Hill
20 unique solo guitar arrangements of rock classics in standard notation and tablature, including: Bohemian Rhapsody • Don't Fear the Reaper • Dust in the Wind • Free Bird • Hotel California • Let It Be • Nights in White Satin • Tears in Heaven • Time in a Bottle • Wonderful Tonight • You Are So Beautiful • and more.
00703633...$14.99

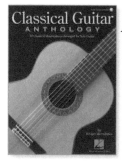

Classical Guitar Anthology
by Bridget Mermikides
Featuring some of the world's most beautiful classical pieces by Bach, Beethoven, Bizet, Dvorak, Greig, Mozart, Puccini, Strauss, Tchaikovsky, Vivaldi, and more, this 32-piece collection also includes traditional guitar repertoire by Albeniz and Tárrega. Includes tab.
00151417 Book/Online Audio $24.99

Classical Guitar Christmas Sheet Music
arr. John Hill
30 top holiday songs are presented in solo guitar arrangements: Away in a Manger • Hallelujah Chorus • I Saw Three Ships • O Little Town of Bethlehem • Silent Night • What Child Is This? • and more. No tab.
00146974...$10.99

The Classical Guitar Compendium
by Bridget Mermikides
This collection features classical guitar technical studies from Sor, Tarrega, Guiliani, Carcassi, and Aguado, as well as presenting fresh guitar arrangements of well-known classical masterpieces. Includes repertoire from Bach, Beethoven, Chopin, Fauré, Massenet, Mozart, Pachelbel, Ravel, Schumann, Tchaikovsky, Wagner and more.
00116836 Book/Online Audio (with tab) $24.99
00151382 Book/Online Audio (no tab)...........$19.99

Classical Guitar Sheet Music
by Bridget Mermikides
Includes 32 masterworks for solo guitar: Alla Hornpipe (Handel) • Ave Verum Corpus (Mozart) • Capricho Arabe (Tarrega) • Dance of the Reed Pipes (Tchaikovsky) • Fantasia No. 7 (Dowland) • Toccata in D Minor (J.S. Bach) • Wedding March (Mendelssohn) • and more.
00280287 Book/Online Audio $24.99

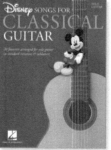

Disney Songs for Classical Guitar
20 songs carefully arranged for solo guitar in standard notation and tablature, including: Beauty and the Beast • Can You Feel the Love Tonight • Colors of the Wind • It's a Small World • So This Is Love (The Cinderella Waltz) • Some Day My Prince Will Come • When You Wish upon a Star • A Whole New World • You'll Be in My Heart • more.
00701753...$17.99

First 50 Baroque Pieces You Should Play on Guitar
ed. John Hill
This one-of-a-kind collection includes selections by Johann Sebastian Bach, Robert de Visée, Ernst Gottlieb Baron, Santiago de Murcia, Antonio Vivaldi, Sylvius Leopold Weiss, and more. Each piece is written in standard notation (no tab) and includes essential right- and left-hand fingerings.
00322567...$14.99

Pop Hits for Classical Guitar
17 expertly crafted guitar arrangements of today's top pop hits written in standard notation and tab, with professional quality audio demonstration tracks performed by a classical guitarist. Songs include: All of Me • City of Stars • Despacito • Game of Thrones • Havana • Hello • Let It Go • Paradise • Royals • This Is Me • A Thousand Years • You Say • and more.
00300506 Book/Online Audio $19.99

Star Wars for Classical Guitar
Music by John Williams
Now classical guitarists can play 14 masterpieces from Star Wars with this collection, including: Cantina Band • Duel of the Fates • Han Solo and the Princess • The Imperial March (Darth Vader's Theme) • The Jedi Steps and Finale • March of the Resistance • Princess Leia's Theme • Rey's Theme • Star Wars (Main Theme) • Yoda's Theme • and more.
00156470...$14.99

The Francisco Tárréga Collection
ed. Paul Henry
Tárrega revolutionized guitar technique and composed a music that will be a cornerstone of classical guitar repertoire for centuries to come. This unique book/audio pack features 14 of his pieces in standard notation and tab: Adelita • Capricho Árabe • Estudio Brillante • Grand Jota • Lágrima • Malagueña • María • Recuerdos de la Alhambra • Tango • and more, plus bios of Tárrega and Henry.
00698993 Book/Online Audio $19.99

HAL•LEONARD®
Order these and more products from your favorite music retailer at
halleonard.com

Disney characters and artwork TM & © 2021 Disney

Prices, contents & availability subject to change without notice.